LEARNING FROM NEW JERSEY

Tim Daly, "The Pulaski Skyway and Route 7," from "Three Weeks in September,"
56" x 113" acrylic on canvas 2003

JOEL LEWIS

LEARNING FROM
NEW JERSEY

with visual works by Tim Daly

Talisman House, Publishers
Jersey City, New Jersey

Manufactured in the United States of America
Printed on acid-free paper

05 06 07 7 6 5 4 3 2 1 FIRST EDITION

Text and titles: Plantin

Book designed by Samuel Retsov

Published in the United States of America by
Talisman House, Publishers
P.O. Box 3157
Jersey City, New Jersey 07303-3157

ISBN: 978-1-58498-056-8

Some of these poems appeared in *Big Bridge, Hanging Loose, Jacket,*
Napalm Health Spa, Long Shot, New American Writing, and
The Outlaw Bible of American Poetry (Thunder's Mouth Press, 1999).
Palookas of the Ozone was published in an earlier version
as a chapbook by e.g. press in 1992.

FOR

George Antheil
Lou Costello
Larry Doby
Allen Ginsberg
Alfred Starr Hamilton
John Marin
Van Dearing Perrine
George Segal
Robert Smithson
Alfred Steiglitz
William Carlos Williams
Larry Young

. . . . native sons

CONTENTS

VISUAL WORKS

Visual works in this book are by Tim Daly. Born and raised in Jersey City and Lake Edenwold, he was infected early by the peculiar charms of Hudson County and the Hackensack River and Meadows. He dropped out of New York's School of Visual arts in 1973 because "Painting was Finished." He lives in Hoboken.

Daly's work is in numerous collections including the Malcolm Forbes Family, writer Nick Tosches, U.S. State Department, Rutgers University, Mark and Esther Villamar, Ruth Walker and Steve Fallon of Hoboken. Commissions to date include the mural series "Three Weeks in September" at New Jersey Transit's Secaucus Junction Rail and a mural painting "Evening, New Brunswick" for the Heldrich Hotel Bar, New Brunswick, New Jersey.

He is represented by DFN Gallery, Chelsea, New York.

"New Jersey — the most American of all states. It has everything from wilderness to the Mafia. All the great things and all the worst, for example, Route 22."

—Jean Shepard

"Strictly speaking, I believe I've never been anywhere."

—Samuel Beckett, "The End"

"Hollywood is not even that great. Hollywood is New Jersey with celebrities."

—Ian Bernardo

"Since I grew up in New Jersey I would say that I was saturated with a consciousness of that place."

—Robert Smithson

LEARNING FROM NEW JERSEY

THE PALISADES: A RUNTHROUGH

for August Kleinzahler

Cartoon details of the scrimshaw skyline
    spread out across James J. Braddock Park.
Who are all those architects? No one gave
    a shit about Raymond Hood except me. I sat
in the bridge tender's shack of my stale life
    dreamt myself up as antic as
Rudy Van Gelder recording miracle music
    only miles away up on Sylvan Avenue.
My days sweating among those neighborly
    foreheads with no rustic footpaths to tread.
The music of night simply women sobbing onto
    worn platters of Joni Mitchell's **Blue.**

So here's the story: no real friends, comrades, disciples
    or lesser associates for leavening.
Now, why did fruit flies buzz above me
    as I walked past the **HOT CARNUBA WAX** Carwash?
What did they exactly do at the building that housed
    PLAYTEX RESEARCH AND DEVELOPMENT?
Why were the massive apartments across from the **Steak n' Shake**
    called the Ponce de Leon Arms?
Every time the TV went on, Walter Cronkite looked at me
    & sneered: *"You did it, you little fucker!"* & he
was right. I wandered Kamena Street seeking telephone nickels
    for the white noise of secret radios.

The memories we're left with are the ones
     we're unable to shake. So say what you want
of human intent, but pizza holds together the social
     better than the illusion of eternity.

Listen up! I'm playing my national anthem for malcontents
     on this Jew's Harp, no bitter rain
here, no humor salvos either. Cliffscapes
     do their thing, eavesdropping
on the Hudson's tidal shifts, absorbing
     the oblique roulette of credits and debits
that's Manhattan's real fossil fuel. Ah (sigh)... our civil
     localized dawn... the Old Ones call it:
Milkman's Matinee.

NORT(H) BERGEN

for Dennis Barone

"Safe Kids" Week?
Boys in flood pants. Seaplane
over Berry's Creek.
Saluggi round-robins. At
the heart of this world:
dreaming confidants.
"Speed jerks. Break
your neck. The undertaker
calls. He wants
you": seen daily
as mystery graffiti. Who's
that doofus up
at Haase's Point? Impacted
Sweet-Tarts. "I'm
Bronco & he's
Flavio!" The event that is
an 8 track cartridge.
Percussive resonance
of a pizza slice. Desert boots.
Crab soccer. Hippie capitalists.
Some even liked
Grand Funk Railroad.
The whole township
was a bulletin. Every
band could play
"Smoke On The Water."

Sauntering towards
the Crazy Crystals.
Boone's Farm
vs. Annie Greensprings:
the apple wine wars.
The haunting profile
of Mr. Snitch. Lorrie Lutz's
name still on the bluestones
of Bull's Ferry Road twelve years
past her graduation.
Look what happened
on Kamena Street! Read
Berrigan, Tom Clark, Lewis Warsh
at 14, thought : DRUGS!
Era of fashionable
panhandling. Three bands:
Juicy Lucy, Blodwyn Pig,
Toe Fat. He was called
"Jake the Gummer"
for undisclosed reasons.
To our amazement, Rufus loved
Little Jimmy Dickens.
GINO'S was not
a Latino Gerontology Center
— it was the home
of the "Gino Giant." The nuances
of flag football. Walking along
Palisades Plaza searching for the latest
issue of Rolling Stone. John Mayall
forms another band. My primal
environment was where the buses

turned around. They beat him up
because he preferred
Rick Wakeman over
Keith Emerson. Live version
of "Inna-Gadda-Da-Vida" with
an even longer drum solo.
Artie Raynes went to
Manhattan courts to challenge
black kids in games
of one-on-one. Winter light
on a White Castle sack. No one
but me remembers
bottlecap baseball. Leonard
spent the day bashing Life Savers
with a sledge hammer. Primitive
marijuana chemistry. Girls
weeping to Joni Mitchell's "Blue".
An informal "Aqualung" study group.
Black arm bands
on Moratorium Day
but not scared Freshman me.
Dreaming of being a free-form,
underground DJ. Moon curdled
above Braddock Park.
Honeker's Dairy on 74th Street.
I resembled Leslie West
back then. I walked
from Nungesser's
to Kamena Street
for the same
reason. Sunset filling

a gas station JFK tumbler.
Young Mayor Mocco singing
"Eve of Destruction"
backed by Tony Cirelli's band.
Canvassing for McGovern voters
at liberal homes filled
with Moses statues. Elephantine
bell bottom pants were
called "elephant bells"
by the wearer. I was at
my lowest ebb on
Kissel Terrace. John Krugnola's
collection of Hitler LPs — *weird* kid.
David Lecin was a fink
for the girls' vice principal.
Frank Steinheimer, future
mortician & friend of John Krugnola,
always in a dark suit. Adult Henry Polio
admitted to me that his young self *really*
did take a shit in a girl's pocketbook.
Every afternoon (1972)
I came home & played
"We're Only In It For The Money"
by the Mothers of Invention. Boys on
local stoops bragging about
Mafia uncles. Sniggering, Franco
called Robyn B.
"The Low-Priced Spread"
& I had no idea
what he meant. Off
to Holthausen's to buy

the Rolling Stone's
"Get Your Ya-Yas Out"
with money I had
panhandled for.
The diner was full of Bronco's
father's scary Croat friends.
A "good job" working
for APA Trucking.
A sack of murderburgers.
Seaplane over Wolf's Creek.
Alvin Lee's one
guitar solo. Saturday
towards Guttenberg.
Too fat
for bodyshirts. Next
step after Grand Funk Railroad:
Bloodrock! Weird blue lights
inside Boucher's Tavern. Teen
drummers' cult worship
of Buddy Rich. Wished for
a lava lamp, a color organ.
Reefer at Incognito Park.
Fleeing from pep rallies.
A Yoo-Hoo at Mezzy's.
Lois Goodman's wardrobe
of earth-tone shifts.
Goodyear blimp
over the backyard. Sue Shore
and her folk guitar.
Speculative days at Nungessers.
Narda L. rumored to

"do it" in the parking lot
at APA Trucking. Vowels take
a beating along the Boulevard.
Air pole socks as worn by
Paulette "Pep" Schneiderman
I was not considered
"a smart Jew". My silent crush
for Kathy Pakluda.
A word always
shrieked in my ear:
"DOUCHEBAGG!!"
The Nesich Brothers' idea
of "fun": taunting
the "retard" Lucien, dishwasher
at Uwe's Luncheonette. Manhattan
Skyline every night through the trees
of Braddock Park.
I raised my hand
when Mrs. Whitehouse
asked: "Who thinks
they're a future
Hemingway?"
— a rare display
of high self-esteem.
We tolerated many
village idiots. Loved
all of John Gunther,
especially Inside USSR.
Engrossed in the LP
cut-out bins. Billy Picca's
daily subordinate sandwich

of Tempte-Whip
on Thomas' date-nut bread. The "h"
in North Bergen is silenced by locals
— *Nort* Bergen. Long reach
of Dan Kelly's Hill Our
principal, Joe Coviello, was one
of Fodham's "Seven Blocks
of Granite" & wept over the P.A.
when friend & teammate Vince Lombardi
died. They called Seid's Luncheonette
"The Chink's" & stole candy from the racks
on their way to class. Boys
in nicotine jackets. Girls on
porches singing Carly Simon.
Bingo lets out. "Susie Q" train whistle
every night at 10:33. Mike's dad
looked forward to Friday's
free clam chowder at Swanee's. Punks
outrunning railroad dicks. No,
I didn't go to "my" prom. Passing
a smiling Bob Sahagian as he
delivered the Daily News. Which
girls "put-out"? — my vicarious
non-sex life. The sky
bleeds above Carlstadt: pollution,
not a miracle. Nungesser's:
a seedy collapsed junction.
Local hero: Boxer Chuck Wepner,
the "Bayonne Bleeder",
pre-Ali. Shell-shocked
"Fatsy-Patsy" Petrillo ranting

at buses — HEY PINKY!!!"
A Hershey's Sky-Hi bar
at Mezzy's. Solace & demerits
at the local library. I thought
men & women smiled
differently. Buy 'em by the sack.

PALOOKAS OF THE OZONE

1.

The art of small city life: it's found
in your posture, an attentive position best
seen astride a bus stop bench.

Think of living in a low place.
Watch factories cool beneath sunset.
Sit down, **please,** & watch things go slant.
Cash flow is a phrase better felt
than understood. Early Atlantic Aretha Franklin pours
out from a Utah Brown 3rd floor condo window.
"I've got just enough for a slice!" — heard much too often
next to Benny Tudino's pizza ovens.

Ah! Pale realism & its invisible rudder moves through
Hoboken's static veins. It's a new moon up there —
Rosh Chodesh — & my wife departs
to that deeper tribe of women.

This night on Washington Street
is my own little theater of patience.

2.

The fatal color of our striving houses
moves across the static
of slang, romance and backfire. Klezmer music
pours out from a window above **Cuba Auto Parts**
making the Visible look the way I like it.

Think of living in a low place.
Somewhere, a door closes just as someone
wakes up, pondering: **"AM I AS <u>BAD</u> AS THAT!?"**
Through a hole the size of a page, phrases drop
out of my speech. Shy Spaniards
sell me semolina loaves
at Policastro's Bakery. And manic sensitivity
won't help. The councilmen are up & about
trolling for voters. Too much time gone by to care
too much about those with smiles & clipboards.

Little shops, close to this house, you are all
richly familiar to me, your stew of tangible gifts.

3.

The true value of Rice-a-Roni is misleading
& the silent nods from passing women
confirms this. Admit, receive, resist,
predict: that train station phone keeps on
ringing. Pale realism & its invisible
rudder. Prowlcars swing into the parking lot
& I perceive exactly who is on the street tonight:
nervous Spaniards with their stale semolina loaves.

"Somebody should just call him **Emil!**" This week
the nomads slept in Little Manila for exotic
and tactile reasons. The average Hobokenite
is 5' 6". Continuing rumors
of a pickpocket school on Garden Street.
There wasn't any rhythm for me in algebra,
so now I'm the Prince of Exits!   America
is its own self-deluding flow chart. Some more
of that red, red stuff. "It" sleeps all morning.

4.

Sophisticated newswomen tell us
how to watch "the war", though certain
stories negate the mordant **CNN**
Newscrawl. Rumors continue
regarding the Garden Street Pickpockets Seminary.
City of continual distortions.
Express train to Port Jervis leaves Hoboken Terminal
five minutes behind schedule.
Solid moon in plain sight.
Power is a luxury for me these
days as I can barely afford
the standard dumpster load
of disempowerment.

I wanted to write you
a political poem, madam: a poem full of that
red, red stuff. But a Sudoku puzzle awaits me
& rain on the bus window maps the wind's direction.

5.

Copcar idling outside of Schaefer's Diner
& the smell of the Maxwell House roasters
stains the snowy air. The setting sun
is a huge Jaffa orange sinking
behind the Watchung Mountains. And the rumble
of the dirty Hudson matches the thud from
a bus rim hitting the bottom of the famous rut
outside Hoboken Terminal. Music begins
where the words leave off. And they call
me: "The Prince of Exits." Oh pale realism!
The luxury of power is played out each day
at the weathered battleship called City Hall. Saying
among painters: "Imitation is the sincerest form
of television." The axis has already tipped
towards the void. Round up the usual literature.
The street bringeth and a bus taketh away.
People outside pointing and staring: business as usual.

6.

Houses and trees in flattened outline,
save one: Ed Foster's House of Poetry, almost glowing
as another issue of Talisman is put to bed. Our city
was to bloom as the Japan of the Rustbelt
— but look what the billboard on City Hall says:
AM I AS BAD AS <u>THAT</u>???   Cash flow
is a phrase better felt than
understood. If there is a narrative here, then it is
the narrative of the failure nexus. The knit brows
of developers put waves in the winds
spilling over the hill we call
Castle Point. And I missed what you wanted to tell me
as boombox roar drowns out the vowels.

Peaceful speedy departure.
Unsteady salutations from a wino's wet brain.
Her interest fades like breath on a mirror.
Paul Motian for president.

7.

It costs a bundle to soundproof against thunder
& it still won't mask the noise of the Saturday
Hoboken revels — that suburb dumbshow played out
in the glow of the Manhattan skyline.
Look: three guys standing on a sewer plate.
Double-parked noisecars stacked by the Blockbusters.
Beerfarts jabbering in peanut-colored weejuns.

In someone's demented version of a rumpus room, the hostess serves
sushi on examples of perfect sentences. Bread truck makes
a speedy departure. Another child support payment
is "forgotten". Power plays in a little room
down the block from Battleship City Hall. We arrived via
the asked-for avenues. The moon is silver scrip
above this pea soup world. Kerouac: "I don't know. I don't
care. And it doesn't make any difference." We go to bed
like anyone else. Blur of Chinese take-out neon on my glasses.

8.

Like dishwater, evening's fresh-minted moon rinsed skylight.
And back on Clinton Street, the **J-Date Anonymous** group sends out
for more coffee. From image to image, the television screen
laughs at me. The luxury of power is played out
every day in every thing. This week the nomads
will pray to the alp at the end of Observer Highway.
I'm painting nothing.

"Have you made up your sputtering mind?????"
The laughter died out on the metallic hell called the Pulaski Skyway.
Was that surrealist stuff or **what?**
Wisdom of my people: "One egg can whiten a bowl of borsht."
The sadness in the old sections of Jersey's towns.
I receive the summer catalog for courses
at the pickpocket seminary. Oh ye ancient gods,
I **salute** your continued silence. Now for a research expedition into
the ordinary night. Jabber what you think. Take me to the bridge.

9.

Welcome to New Jersey: in a friend's jalopy, driving
along Piaget Avenue to a pizza joint listening
to Led Zeppelin's "When The Levee Breaks"
on a cassette deck. Now **that's** social realism. Difficult
to recall this local air, but I know it's Hoboken
because evening's haze is magnetic. And it gets so
warm this mid-February that I think
out loud: "It's like a day in spring… **which is when
my unemployment runs out!"** Hey moneygrip! What **is**
the role of profane objects? I arrived through the courtesy
of asked-for boulevards. Cash flow is a phrase better
felt than understood. It is time to introduce
the pioneers of the five-fingered discount. *He* remembers
the **Bizzaros** & their cubed inverted planet.

Darkness is apparent as coins jingle in this conventional city.
My overriding young ambition was to be overlooked.
"Whole Lotta Love": soundtrack of my high school years.

10.

People that enjoy echoes ... well, they're just
bumping their mothers. What goes on
inside the mind of the countermen
of Policastro's Bakery? It isn't "memory"
that keeps me in this landscape. I would like you
to meet Cecilia Buxt, the Kinsey Professor
of Soul Food Analysis at Stevens Tech.
Who's at home? Let's walk these streets
& find out. Remember, one egg can whiten
a whole bowl of borsht.

Beer farts keep on jabbering. I will return
to my point of departure and will find
my heart in the honesty of women. No army
wears a different uniform. Noisy night air
overloaded with the transcript of the dreams
of the disempowered. The mirage maps are torn.
If this is a failure nexus, then it is a narrative.

11.

Graffiti on the train station wall: "Just say **NO** to tuna!"

Are you ready for Dharma Combat, lotus brain?
We bus passengers are detained by pothole excavations.
With packs of Kools from the newest merchant
from the sub-continent, the teen gang is ready for a night
of yelps, street puking and discussions of the course offerings
at the Clinton Street Pickpockets Seminary. They sell moon-in-a-tube
on Newark Street — "just like our soldiers in Iraq see
every night." And for those who can't bother with
houseplants: plush toy ferrets. I'm painting nothing again.
I salute your silence, *asshole*. Would you like me to put
the coffee together? The bums went out traveling
incognito, donning the nightshirts
of ordinary sleep. And instinctively, we whisper in both
museums and banks. Inhabiting the morning
with my complications. Salutations from a wet brain.

12.

It's a small chink from the waxed canopy of mindless
patriotism — surplus flag waving used as talisman
against fears of what might be up ahead.

How did we arrive at these conclusions?
The American dead were covered in silver blankets.
Saddam Hussein had a fondness for Doritos.
We fake an interest in our own affairs.
How did the term "cry uncle" come about? Nervous
citizens of Hoboken go about their daily errands
with an air of raw nostalgia. Hello, George the mailman.
Malcolm, pass me that Boonton Line schedule. People tend
to be hostile after a heavy lunch. Camille Paglia, professional
crazy academic, calls the male urination stream:
"An arc of transcendence."

Hard to specify what is desired from this
picture book of fake needs. We go to bed
like anyone else. Picasso: "When I haven't any blue I use red."

13.

*I promise you, the world goes on
while you sleep.* And day-by-day, we are ruled
by the colorless murmur of schwa, in full plumage
as inverted "e". My wife wakes from sleep
shrieking: *"I dreamt that my down coat was possessed!"*
And isn't that such a *small* price for participating
in the history of the world. We fake interest
in our social transactions. I'm painting nothing.

And beer farts keep on jabbering, now All-American
yahoos of a New World Order. Their
laughter fell to white noise as they
entered the metal hell called "Pulaski Skyway."
I salute their silence. Slick newscasters
prepare us for peace and plenty.
Some more of that red, red stuff. Solid metallic
moon in plain sight. Oh *please* let me dance
to the tension of a world on the wane.

IN HOBOKEN (WINTER)

1.

The Empire State Building
glows blue and white
tonight — **Happy Channukah!**—
thanks to a little girl's letter
that melted owner Leona Helmsley's
blue-ice heart

& in the festival's spirit, all
I can say to all you modern Assyrians is:
"You ain't *gonna* Hellenize me!"

2.

Here's that women I've seen
on Hoboken's streets for years. **Man,**
is she tough looking! *"An imposing
women"*, says my wife. I'd like to ask her
what she does for a living
but I'm afraid she'd sew
my ass to my lips
& laugh it about it, later.

3.

The overpriced restaurant
is empty again tonight.

The bored waitstaff has
run out of exotic locales to
daydream about.

4.

Here comes
the Eleanor Roosevelt
of Hoboken striding
out of the Farmboy.

I see her new protest pin which
equals a new local crisis which
equals a clipboard
heavy with petitions.

I think: **"No turban walks
the Western floor"**
& dash across Washington Street.

5. At The Pamrapo Bank, Washington Street

The guy ahead of me
slammed his fist
into the A.T. M.
"FUCKING MACHINE!"

His girlfriend said:
*"Don't worry, I got
money."*

He said:
"Nah, I didn't **need** no money.
I just **wanted** money."

6. Mars Poetica

I take my stand here
though no one reads
my "Jersey" poems
here in New Jersey.

I'm exotic as goat turds
but not as profound.

7. To Sinatra

I pass your birthplace
Chairman, now a vacant lot
on Monroe Street
& wonder
if you'd like my poetry
or would you just see me
as that sort of artsy slob
you'd love to beat up
that kind of guy who'd yawn
in front of a woman.

8.

Hearing Coltrane
in the headphones
allows me some belief
in the transcendent
as the Hudson Place A.T.M.
swallows my MAC card.

9. River Street

What's happening
on the other
side of this
corner?

Frat habits
subdued at
the Tech
Institute in old
brownstones

that maitain old
school dignity.
Men walk past
eating Cheetos
thinking old
songs that made

them happy.
The coffee factory
abandoned, dark.
Lone Moran tug

stirs up
the Hudson
scrambling reflected
Manhattan lights.

New signage downtown:
Red umbrella
of the Travelers Group

irks Tribeca gentry
spiritually uplifts this
urban Jersey boy.

My emotional weather
gets clocked as "steady"
beneath the indicating hand
of the Clam Broth House.

10. For Che' Guevara

Local punks
don't punch
out windows
of fancy cars
anymore. It's

not that class
hatred no longer
fills their hearts.
Those boys

sailed to a land
where they latch ties
onto broadcloth shirts

& burn off that rage
face-painted looney
at **Jersey Devils** games.

11. In My Dotage

Young people
on Hoboken streets
looking like
college friends
not seen
in years.

12.

Call me lentil.
Don't call me
"professor"
or "Rock Bottom".
My pockets aren't
bottomless.
This is the untrue
magnetic west.
Tugboat captains
call the Hudson
"North River"
while it sloshes
past Manhattan, but
I call it "Izzy"
from my vantage
at Castle Point.

It seems
every time
I think
I weaken
this nation. Maybe
it's an improvement,
maybe an unconscious
gesture of reconciliation
from this lapsed
anarcho-syndicalist.

13.

"MEA CULPA!"
says the gum spot
beneath my Keds.

"I know how you feel",
I reply, dragging my ass
to the PATH station.

LEARNING FROM NEW JERSEY

for Robert Smithson

Rogue meteorologists call it a "radium sunset" but the air
always shouts out someone's Christian name, the braying voice
of Saint Springsteen drifts from the swirl
of tactile local daydreams.

I negotiate a Hot Texas Weiner at Libby's — just north
of the Great Falls of the Passaic River.
"Talk as if you love truck noise," sez the douchebag
to my left. So I fart propel myself off this tan

counter stool, clocks on the street reading
in fascistic digital output, the night-carved river slush,
ears outsized in search of a quarry & so what's up, ghostie men?
Doc Williams boats: "I love oncoming traffic!"

A new-old place created by different circumstances. And just
how much chump change is left for a bus to Newark's
authentic Tibetan altar? *Just enough.* And at your local
abandoned bijou: "Shlolmo and His Mendicants"... LIVE!

Events are sensational here at the dinner. My local
Hagstrom map is unencumbered by personal choice
while day after day, my "poetic eye" is rewarded
with some big mutt's steaming heap on my shoes.

A battered UFO lands in North Bergen, but no one notices.
At the Crooks Avenue Flea Market, meta-fictioneers
sell their unpublished novels by the kilo. Dusk
and smoke signals appear atop the Ramapo Mountains...

Indians? Or a brush fire at the Vegetal Cleave
State Park's rest stop? Pick up the House of Jersey
& see what crawls out — WHAT'S **THAT?** Sounds like..
The Gettysburg Address in Pig Latin?? ... more consideration

than the brain contains. Useful golems trail me
into the defiles of Great Notch then down
to Ong's Hat and back upstate for an update
on the wise men of Wanaque and Succasunna.

I haven't a clue or a farthing; I'm just a manjerk
in a mortgaged land. "My bowel movements
are the pliable substance of disastrous thought,"
says the detenured professor stacking Cheese-Nips

at the village salumeria. The "line" is the first thing
to go as the poet ages. Hear the locals snicker
as I wobble along New Jersey Railroad Avenue
looking for something I didn't loose.

Now I hear the faint jangle of bangled wrists blend
with the primordial boogie-woogie of Albert Ammons
and now it rains with a gentle hiss — *ah,* lovely
Overpeck Creek where the torrent shrinks to a soodling thread.

Hey, check my pants pockets — **ZIP!** And
across the street: a white man turns grey
against the neon rainbow spiral sign
of Passaic's Quisqueya Bar.

I wish I didn't have to think these "things"
cease further casual combinations of pronouns
& go back, finish up my MA at the Lockpicker's Seminary.
What's looming? Nothing's looming! Slagball of capitalism

keeps-a rolling as I down a 3rd Dunkacinno while
Howling Wolf sings "Smokestack Lightning"
for the sake of a featureless humanity. I fail again
at blowing smoke rings. A boy just watches me, winces.

I check my Golem into a pet motel & get back on
another bus, cargo pants heavy with vended delicacies.
Sunset colors anticipate my drift but you
are my strangers and I have written through fog for you.

........LEAVE THE CANNOLI

for David Chase

"I equate John [Gotti] as a real stand-up true believer. He went to jail and died. ...... There were more gangland killings from 1985 to 1992 than in the history of the country. Then it became almost a joke, a metaphor, and HBO came along: **The Sopranos.** The actors, I know them, and they're great people, but what they're portraying is the *lowest* form of life. There's not a single redeeming character, not a single person with *respect*. Not even the psychiatrist — she doesn't have respect for herself. Except — that one Sicilian kid, with the ponytail, he had a little bit of respect, and then he went running back. They're just fat, *greedy*, foulmouthed *lowlifes*. The Sicilian kid — he had a crush on the wife, I think — he was the one character that I thought had a little dignity in him. And the Russian girl, who lost her leg, and who worked so hard."

—Bruce Cutler, John Gotti's long time attorney, from "Kiss City," by Ben McGrath, *The New Yorker*, 5/1/06

1.

I called
your **fucking**
house five
times yesterday!

Now, if you're going
to disregard
my **motherfucking**
phone calls

I'll blow **you**
and that **fucking** house **up**!

This is not a **fucking** game!

My **time** is valuable!

... and if I ever hear that **anybody**
else calls you & that you
responded within five days,
... I'll fucking kill you!

2.

A Major Life Lesson:

On an East New York stoop
watching wise guys
in pearl-gray gingerella hats
leavlng from home at noon in
Twizzler black Caddys

— while his working stiff neighbors
carried baloney sandwiches
onto the BMT trains.

3.

You tell this punk:

I,
me,
John Gotti

will
sever
your
head
off!

4.

All I want is a good sandwich.

You see this sandwich here?
This tuna sandwich?

Thats all I want
— a good sandwich.

5.

My fucking father
was born in New Jersey.

He ain't been in Italy
his whole fucking life
— my mother neither!

The guy never worked a
fucking day in his life!

He was a rolling stone.

He never provided for the family.

He never did <u>nothing.</u>

He never earned **nothing.**

And we never had **<u>nothing!</u>**

6.

Restauranteur Luigi Nanni
would have Gotti's
favorite fish, branzino,
flown in from Milan.

The Teflon Don
liked it prepared
in a cast-iron skillet
with just olive oil,
herbs and sea salt.

Gotti insisted
that the fish
had to be alive
when it arrived
at Nanni's, unlike
the dead, NY Post-wrapped
local fish that landed
on the stoops
of Gotti's enemies.

7.

I Don't Deal With This Anymore

> *Standing on a street corner*
> *waiting for no one is power.*
> —— *G. Corso*

I tell them: Listen! Your
skipper will keep me
up to date, you keep
your skipper up to date.

I can't socialize with these guys.
I can't bring myself down.
I'm a boss — *you know what I mean?*

I gotta isolate myself
a little bit..

8.

OMERTÀ

I could have robbed
a church
but I wouldn't admit
to it even
if I had
a steeple
sticking out
of my ass.

9.

On Greed & its Consequences

That's not John Gotti.
At least, I hope
that's not me. Maybe
I see myself in a light
that I'm not in
.... I don't know.

10.

Life: A User's Manual

A man
who
does not
gamble
has no
compassion.

"Joy Ride Chevy, Ravine Road, Jersey City," 8.5" x 12", acrylic on muslin, 2006,
Private collection.

TACHOGRAPHY/SHORTHAND/
QUICKWRITING

"All the visible world is nothing but a shop of images and signs."
—Charles Baudelaine

Approaching the magnificent verdure
of Staten Island

I spill ice coffee
over an open seat

the cranky cleaning guy
sneers: "Thanks a <u>lot</u>, **MISTER!**"

but I won't say: **"Its clumsy slobs like me
that gives meaning to your labors!"**

instead, yell out: "Hey man, I'm sorry!"
& dash off the ferryboat.

    ❧❧❧❧

"A happy poet is not a good poet"
says Konstantin K. Kuzaminsky, the unhappy
Russian avant-gardist in the exile hell
of fast-food America.

Reading about the poet and the devotees who keep him
in black bread, slivovitz and Kents, it appears that this big,
bearded, bathrobbed poet is merely the Buddha's decision
to return Ted Berrigan to this world of Samsara.

꿿꿿

Nursing student Elizabeth Jordan
discovered herself deep in a world of shit
one morning on the L.I.E.
when the stuck accelerator
on her Chevy Blazer turned it
into an 85 mph rush hour bullet.

Calling **911** on her cell phone,
she was told not to hyperventilate
and stay calm. The dispatcher then
asked: *"Have you downshifted?"*

"Downshifted into what!," replied
Jordan, trying not to cry,
"I'm a female, I'm sorry."

꿿꿿

Interviewer: Is it possible to be happy being alone?

Merril Markoe: "It's possible but its difficult. Though I made a point in
teaching myself how to do it."

Interviewer: What are the rules?

Markoe: "Get over it! You're not the center of the world! Who's looking at you? And if they are, big deal! It's not such a big fucking deal! You're not under a building in Turkey!"

❧

A tractor-trailer
crashed on the interstate
spilling its fuel
& a payload of broccoli
all over the asphalt.

The ensuing fire was so big
that authorities thought
a plane had crashed
when they arrived
on the scene.

"Holy Shit! " said fire fighter Brad Reist,
"There was steamed broccoli
all over 81."

❧❧❧

Harbor loaded
      with tugs
& while Jack DeJohnette
      solders the hole in my head
I look out towards
      Kill Van Kull
searching for a Chevron oil tanker,
    The S.S. Condoleezza Rice.

So, who does have "the money"
      on this
earthly paradise?

      ❧❧❧

A man who underwent
13 laser surgeries
to have a misspelled tattoo removed
has settled a lawsuit for $7,000
against the shop
where he got it, **Body Art World**
of Seaside Heights, NJ.

In 1999, Joseph Beahm got a tattoo
showing a knife stabbing
into a man's back, with the words:
"WHY NOT, EVERYONE ELSE DOES."

The word *else* was spelled
"e-l-e-s-e".

&

&&&

&

A group of Hasidic Jews
have bought land near Amherst, Massachusetts
attempting to recover the culture of their ancestors
by starting America's first kosher organic farm.

Is there some inherent conflict
between piety & technology?

One pioneer, Shmuel Simenowitz, notes:
"There's a story about a man who kept praying,
'God let me win the Lotto. *Ha Shem*, please let me
win the lotto' and finally God says, 'It would help
if you bought a ticket.'

You see,
we believe in divine providence, but that's no
substitute for skills. God will give you the miracles,
but he first wants to see the business plan."

&&&

No reveries,
cousin. And my thoughts
shift
to the blue ice
of Mars
then back
to a normal flannel
in the daily filtration
of street furniture,
factoids & brief
human interactions.

Call it "Silly Putty planet"
and no one would be
indignant. Evening news'
grim male faces
interrupted by
its mirror: ads
for adult diapers.
Stan Getz has returned
to judge the world
but needs his Camels
& a single malt Scotch
to get straight. He ain't no
wrathful deity, really. So,

in between the Atlas
of Good and Evil, there's
a high lonesome sound that
stands in for the general lack
of things we are

invested in. You see,
I'm the guy
who inspired the phrase:
"Doesn't get along well
with others."

ຈ຺

The late ethnomusicologist Alan Lomax
created the Global Jukebox, a vast database
of songs and dances cross-referenced
with anthropological data. His pioneering work
continues on at Hunter College's
Association for Cultural Equity.

"We now have cultural machines
so powerful that one singer
can reach everybody in the world,
& make all the other singers feel inferior
because they're not like him," Lomax noted
at the end of his life.

"Once that gets started, he gets backed
by so much cash & so much power that
he becomes a monstrous invader
from outer space
crushing the life
out of all human possibilities.

My life has been devoted
to opposing that tendency."

੭ઙ੭ઙ

The Trentonian's Tony Persichilli
insists that he wasn't trying
to get some cheap laughs
at the expense of the mentally ill
when he chose to caption
a story about a 3-alarm blaze
at the Trenton Psychiatric Hospital
with the headline:
ROASTED NUTS

"When I wrote it", claims
the NJ editor, "I didn't intend
to hurt anybody's feelings, upset
anyone's sensibilities or make fun
of anybody's handicaps."

੭ઙ੭ઙ

Upper New York Bay was smooth enough
to Xerox, a vast marbled endpaper
freckled with the turds
of underserved Brooklyn. And I won't
shout out: "Dark coffee of the sea!", but
who am I really kidding?

Just use klieg lights in the victim's absence.
The still trees of Battery Park
tell the gulls to quit daydreaming. The magic
in losing money in the street
equals the pleasure of spraying for crane flies
in a South Carolina factory.

A pleasant proposition? Got me.
I remain stormy in this paradise.

&

According to a new study published
by the National Academy of Science

the female brain is wired
to feel emotions more intensely
& remember them more vividly.

Women who participated in the study
got more upset, for longer, than
male subjects after being shown
pictures of dead bodies, gravestones,
crying people & dirty toilets.

&

I INTERVIEW SONNY ROLLINS

Mr. Rollins, you've known so many
of the giants of jazz — Miles, Bird,
Monk, Trane, Brownie —
Do they ever visit you in your dreams?

       Yes, they do.

What are they doing?

               Oh, they're just hanging around, doing
the same sort of things they did when they were alive.

Do they say anything to you — messages from the beyond?

No, it's just like watching old-time home movies.
But my mother, she's **always** giving me
advice in my dreams. You know
how **that** is, don't you?

     ﻊ

 A bearded man walked into
the main branch
of the Kansas City library
wanting to pay
the outstanding late fees
of every card-holder
named Mohammed.

When a perplexed & mistrustful librarian
refused his VISA card
the hirsute samaritan took care
of 600 dollars worth of fines
with 600 packages
of low-sodium Ramen noodles.

It turned out the library was holding its
annual "Tardy Food Drive" in which
book scofflaws can erase a dollar of debt
with each nonperishable item.

Branch manager Gretchen Dombrock
declared: "I've never seen so many
packages of Ramen noodles!"

&

Gus Long
sought to develop
new sources of oil
in the Western Hemisphere
to reduce dependence
on the Middle East.

To that end he oversaw
Texaco's operations
in Trinidad, Venezuela
& Canada.

"Gus Long was a great builder at a time
of rapid expansion after WWII," said
James W. Kinnear, his successor as
CEO of Texaco.

Mr. Kinnear said he often tried to emulate
Mr. Long's oratorical style
in motivating his own sales staff
— with little success.

"He was basically a marketer,"
Mr. Kinnear said. "He used to come
to sales meetings
& recite poetry.

He'd get you **so** stirred up."

NORTH JERSEY
ASHKENAZIC
ANTI-SZYGY

MY POETRY INDUCES ACID REFLUX

On leave from
the spam wars, I
get down to business
& price the bright
occupations
lurking in money's
gateway.

So, sure, my brain
is in foster care
but my forkball is sharp
and my dowsing stick gets
me about the famished
soil of Garrett Mountain.

After all, I'm describing
a simple mechanism
and here at the Accidental Blank Spot
I stand cattycorner
with Jehovah's Witnesses
and fake Rolex vendors
trying to hawk irony
from the back end
of a bread truck.

So, don't cry for me errant radio waves —
it's a calenderish thing
untouched by river men. Here,
at the site of No Power
you don't need a cop
you don't need a hit man
you don't need a shaman
but you **do** need a bookie.

Suction prints
from my flip-flops
leave a trace on this
magnetic dust. And
the distance between
putative author
and suspect reader
lends enchantment
to the remnants
of Paterson's lone
greeting card shop.

FILIBUSTERING IN SEACACUS

I sold my language
at a flea market
and the small talk here

on Paterson Plank Road
is a conception vessel
for the native inertia.

I sit weightless in a bus shelter
with waffles in the pockets
and Ruth Brown
up from my i-Pod.

PASSING THE TUBE BAR (shuttered)

Twilight Journal Square
    of noise cars
    small appliances
    99 cents shops
    Boulevard Franks
    & stains that won't go away

'72 back-flash to the abundant dais
of the Victor Hotel
the idealistic McGovern babe boy
got a Moe-sized face slap
on the brain of his body politic
watching local elected crooks carve
chunks from the national pie.

Dreams of summer band concerts
& efficient snowstorm removal
haunt him now.

The simple republic
and livable agora
all nailed to that background.

IN THE ABSENCE OF THEIR SURPRISE

I help a Peruvian family
find their way
to hometown North Bergen
walking them over
to the Journal Square trains
            but I'm not sure if they really trust me
swaddled in cargo pants, fanny pack
& a Klezmatics t-shirt

Right now,
the PATH train
is a mobile icebox
of relaxed weekend faces
as we pass a meadow estuary
filled with people eating cheesecakes
who have forgotten their official histories
            & when night drops
those ex-goat herders start bonfires, play
pool checkers & sing wistful camp songs
of the proto-Khazars
            & on the south bank of the Second River
a team of outlaw botanists
determine acceptable habitations
and read from the Book of Daylight for comfort.

            I marvel at the flexibility of the random
days purchased as a hedge fund. And

where have you, You & YOU gone,
friendly faces that once
populated my life?

All the social lies
spoken on these Hoboken streets
soldered together by bits
of strained social theories.

What can I ask from you
that I can barely expect
from myself?

Back home and up above
Washington Street's curbs,
I watch the night world.

AFTER HUGH MACDIARMID

New Jersey! Everything he saw in it
was a murderburger he held in his brain,
both sides steam-cooked at once.

He tried to saddle
the contradictions between
the dream of a world language
and the Jimmies vs. Sprinkles debate that
splits the ice cream eaters
of south and north jersey.

He couldn't.
Reluctantly, he returned to his satellite radio
and thought hard about the longitudinal bias
of the **New Jersey Transit** bus pass.

Absorb the local lilt
now fading away
from the body blows
of both rich
and indigent
transients.

I remember
how an old longshoremen
ended an anecdote
about a bar room brawl
on Hoboken's ghost Barbary Coast
with an animated
"them wuz the days!"
in front of the Hudson Place taxi stand

I believed him absolutely:
hallucinations are increasingly verbal.

I forgot time while in Bayonne.
My inner chronoscope did not
return until days later
while dreaming of brown men
smoking clove cigarettes.

That beautiful concert of the abstract
changed my attitude twice
and gave me the urge
for going back
to dear Oil City.

Going thru the Hudson Tubes again:
a man reads a diary of crushed things.
A women and her Geiger counter.

Jersey is out of work.
Tofutti nears the mouth.
The "great man theory" is solvent.

We are going east
threading Morton Street
on the fancy side of the Hudson.
My left hand grips that
Bromo Seltzer blue umbrella.

My old heart was puked on all
over in Metuchen. It was my own
fault, side-trucking with
a donut for a brain, bit player
under indictment, stoop dweller
2 am waiting
a milk truck just
goofing
in the extremes
of all my tales.

Pleading before
some elusive magistrate, my
posse was late in arriving
and my troglodyte manners
took center stage.

Oh, palookas of the ozone —
what do I owe you in tips?
Hand jive is not working, I'll
wing it in Esperanto!

CRINKLING MOJO

I'm back on
Boulevard East
again, a beehive
in the backpack
& seltzer squishing
in my shoes

Across the Hudson
there is nothing
but the methadone called money
and numbing neon the opposite
of steel.

Still. no better business than
one's own inattention
to the pay stub geek. Cars go by
bearing hip-hop's tag
cracking the night's cement.

I'll call in to the operator
requesting sleep. Jersey's refueled
skeeters sailing out towards
the city of occupied lights.

SHELF LIFE

Truth, the old ones say,
is an apartment of components.
So count me out of that loop, because
I'm the Charlie Rouse
of the soul. And my vast library
of inscribed chapbooks
is as useless as monkey farts
as I face off daily
with the actual mechanics of money.

Poetry is not a hobby, it is a.....
Uh....... It's like,,,, uh...uh....
....Oh....

                    Meanwhile,
back in Bayonne, emotionally
troubled cashiers ring up
Chilean cantaloupes. *All forms*
wait for their full language.
$1.25, **please.**

DURING THE ADMINISTRATION
OF GOVERNOR BRENDAN BYRNE

for Ed Smith

My fried calamari Special is as tasty
as Ray-O-Vac batteries
as this Botany Village bistro
is lashed by a summer storm.
Trouble in the East? That don't
confront us. We're ashamed
to compare pay stubs and order
tap water with zero appetizers
to shrink the tab. Words. Women.
Baseball. Music. Welcome
to 1975 & we're immunized
courtesy of the anti-disco vaccine.

Our marching orders are yet
to be revealed, but golden birdies
whisper about the tremendous sadness
below the Watchungs demanding
our documentation. We're
too dumb to smoke, settle for toothpicks,
and flee in the wake
of our minimalist tip.

Later, you point your piece-of-shit Mustang
onto dear Route Three, destination: **out**
& onto a stool at Rutt's Hut.
Corn relish is all we need
to correct the night's mistakes.

SMALL RANT

The nation's bad weather is not my fault though
it happened on my watch, but everything happens
on my watch and George W. Busch wants to
burn my ass about it — I hear him snarling out there.

Everyone wants good dreams. No one wants to feel
stupid, "out of it", or a member of no clique, but
we do. No one wants to strip search the couch
for bus fare, but it happens everyday.

How wonderful to be in the arms of cerebral creatures.
You'll never know what hand you'll get dealt, so
put down that baloney sandwich and listen up! The very
floodlit lights of heaven has been leased — *deal with it!*

I'd like to think I'm on an island, but I'm hardly
a Magellan kind of guy. I think I hear Shirley Bassey singing.

CREDO IN US

The old revolutionary dreamworld turns
to goofer dust & as for me:
no inner life at all. My group home kids
affectionately call me "White Motherfucker"
& they're 50% right. While looking
for a central committee that would
have me, the Ukrainian woman
gently assured me: "There's no Chicken Kiev
in Kiev!" — one quandary solved,
three zillion to go.

Dishes in the sink, 3 am.
& add to that: a fat bag of laundry
& the cold corrosive touch
of reality tv. In my taboret,
there's some letterhead, two Malcom X stamps,
a few rubber bands
& not a single flag

NORTH JERSEY ASHKENAZIC ANTI-SZYGY

Smithson gave me clues
not Ginsberg
    Williams
      Springsteen
      Bon Jovi
        or
      Baraka

on how to safely ingest
this zed landscape
& quarry the crystals
beneath the floorboard.

So what do I owe
to Hendrick's Causeway
for my moral development?
Does it matter?
    or should I have gone
to a pick-pocket's school
instead of Naropa, back in '81?

Maybe I have romanticized
& idealized my geography
      & that the comment : *"Reading your*
poetry is like a guided tour
of New Jersey in a old jalopy!"
is more cautionary prescriptive
than praise song.

Tonight's Tonnelle Avenue
is a damaged ribbon in
shades of Sabretts.
The earnest workers
of the Philippine Desiccated Coconut Company
await the Hackensack bus
clutching Statue of Liberty dolls
singing songs
of the Turnpike
and of the elevators
that take them to their
heated green apartments
in neighborhoods
whose ballrooms and bijous
are turned into body shops.

On my side of the Palisades
is the toney shtetl
called Hoboken where
my brain functions
like an interesting sewer
deriving energy
from the complex vision
of both Huntz Hall
& Curly Howard.

Now what does one do with
this enormous gift of time?
—— to become a dreary consumer sponge
or devote a blog to equivalents
of nose hair and naval lint?

I'll call my new words "Dark Scouts".
& put on Albert Ayler to patrol
the premises. The new street lamps
puts a bright color on people's faces
— does it make us aware of ourselves
as humans with specific histories?
— or is part of a circuit touched off
by everything we see, hear,
evaluate or just want to do.

Tim Daly, "Southwest View From the Wittpenn Bridge," 36" x 72", acrylic on canvas, 2003. Collection of Mark and Esther Villamar, Hoboken, N.J.

COMPENSATION PORTRAIT

The silk factories have
burned down. The people
live in isolate
huts. The mayor has gone
home to Boonton. The beauty school
is issuing traffic tickets.
The drinking water is wounded.
The Great Falls seeks another
path. Chump change hits
the curb & no one
picks it up.
Mormons are on Market Street
selling their Pearl
of Great Price. Pay phone
ringing in the Ward Street parking lot.
Your friends have fled
Paterson. No squirrels. Someone
begins an essay on concrete.
Did you get the money we sent?
Empty apartments. A jalopy
in need of a new radiator hose.
The old circus hotel burns
down. No money for gas, so the taxis
run on static. Ghostly tongues of water
throughout the evening.
The potato chip vendors
war with one another.

Up *there* are the Second Watchungs.
A Buick drops into a pothole. Dirty
statues. Did you get the money
we sent? A nameless
uncarved block stands in
for your future. Paterson
is a relay of false
and true alarms. The moon
is not a thin silent key.

In your head: sea storm, a nor'easter.
A chilidog squirts out of its bun
and lands on the sidewalk
of Ellison Street.
This is **not**
an experiment
in the American
idiom. What
did one do
in Paterson,
1955? **Get**
the MONEY!!
A library
is burning
down. Black-out
& "friends"-turned-thieves
have redecorated
your loft through
attrition. Did you get
the money we
sent you? Look up,

are those tangrams
of tint moonlight
or just street lamp
glare? Drunken wanderings
through a midnight
housing project. It has
gone beyond peculiar
personal habits.

Just enough
for a chilidog, maybe
a birch beer. On the shirt side
of this street, nothing
looks like homes. A snatch
of Jethro Tull from
a passing blue Subaru
snaps me back
to an easier way
of telling this. New rain
Kool-Whips West Broadway's
ripe debris. What is a mojo? Can
you pick up the house? A mailbox
is on fire. No one believes you
any more. A pizza shop radio blares
inevitable "oldies". Sidewalks
obliterated by black gum spots.
A hot dog cart explodes. *Did you get
the money we sent?* Coffee
is not drunk
by mendicants.
What does

one do
in Paterson
circa 1997?
— DUCK!!
The children's toys
are burning. Empty bus
deadheads
to the Market Street garage.
You've become
the man your
father was. Did you get
the money we sent?
Your life — the open window.

ANHEDONIA

SHIFT IN THE WINDS

1.

Monday, sat inside Newark Street's ex-bank
Starbucks, drank espresso macchiato
& paid for it with my Walt Whitman
Starbucks Debit Card *"Here is not*

> *merely a nation*
> *but a teeming*
> *nation of nations."*

Poor Walt, out of copyright & now serving
the interests of orchestrated leisure time.

                    It's the day before autumn, cool.
Women lug behemoth purses. A gagglet
of girls heading off to the soccer pitch. The last
old men of Hoboken ruminate
at the Wilton House tavern

                    listlessly?

or with old-time genial mood,
those chiseled Adriatic faces
& a cane propped against the worn mahogany bar.

      No more vaudeville houses   No more dock work
      No more Lackawanna train crews upstairs at the Hotel Victor.

To the affluent go the spoils.

2.

Tuesday evening, Danny, Joey,
Deb & I discuss the possibility
of writing some **really** good
political poetry. *"Blows*

against the empire!"
says Danny. *"How about a poetry*
the equivalent to a room clearing
fart against the ***POWER***,*"* I suggest.

We then left
for separate stations. Late at night,
a call from Joey: **"I am beset by flies!"**
e-mail from Deb: *"The heavy secret*
lie *of the heart is by far*
the most interesting subject."

3.

This tiny world, self-reflected
into a gentle take on entropy.

The remnants of the late hurricane
dusts Washington Street's pizzerias and realtors.

The rogue electricians return
from their rounds   The line

grows at the lottery machine peopled by
folks eager for a paradise

in an empire of repose. Human
me, shaking off Old World time

to repair the blunt force
of circumstance. Daydreams

dictate my holidays.

Patch in the warm associations.

Load the **U-Haul** with used aggregate

... & emerge from the Holland Tunnel
and visit the **House of One's Own Mistakes**
in a waterfront town opposite
the city of occupied lights.

We spend a night talking about
the fate of dear, dead Paterson
in this post-Doc Williams world.
          and as the linguine gets passed around
the sympathetic talk is of friends
in the outer orbits of our lives.

*"Sheer happiness in an unshaken mind
is more than most of us hope for."*

Here I am here — sitting on the floor, grinding my
teeth, alphabetizing my CDs
by the name of the sound engineer. So,
                                    this goes out to you Rudy Van Gelder,
acoustic maestro.

                              ❧❧❧❧❧❧

The Talmud warns: "Keep away the multitudes from your house.
<u>Do</u> **not** <u>**bring**</u> everyone to your house!"   Nerves flayed
by reality TV stampede.
                              I see two policemen sauntering down
Clinton Street ready to challenge me to Parcheesi.

My salad fork catches fire but I still
plan to read the headlines. Our mayor's hair:
the shade of a radioactive eggplant.

Midnight:

the Buffalo Poetics List
is available.

I scroll the digest
searching for
an interesting
thread

as a car alarm gets
set off by a roving
garbage truck.

The absolute bureaucracy of size
& obsolescence has me
whipped. The telegraph is antique.
Pneumatic tubes still whip beneath Paris streets on
pure inertia. Princess phones? Wire Paladin??

                                        Separated by one second
I no longer see the "I" in "us". Salute a flag or be branded
TRAITOR.   Dysthymia relieved by the writing
of poetry?   Memory-driven
baked apple smell out the diner door. Keith Richards sneers:
*"Led Zeppelin was a project — not a **band!**"*
Who knew?

Lee Konitz as the perennial underachiever, though
as "pure" an improviser as we got.

"Oh no! Another Virtuoso!" — his sly putdown & shout out to all those
leather-lung Maynard Ferguson-types, **or** how much
virtuosity is too much virtuosity?

> *"Fortunately for me,"* he declares in **Motion**'s liner notes,
> *"I never really made it professionally, so I've had the chance
> to relax & get a little insight into my life."*

All is pure.   Command of space. Just walking, expecting
nothing in this light snow.

I wasn't a Messianic fink
eating lungen stew back then
nor do I hope that's my
gig in the *World-to-Come*.

We invent ourselves
out of the sawdust from
a butcher shop we don't own
— a process absent facts

and what **can't** be reproduced
is a sense of absolute presence.
— no glory dream of the glowing wreath.
         . . . and I ain't no APR cover boy

or grant recipient calculating interest.
"Brainless as a biscuit" could be
the social diagnosis. I pencil in the days
when I have time to sail out of my head.

AUTOTOPOGRAPHY

Where can I launder my money tonight?

> No luster on this
> waterfront   *"Whatever happened*
> *to Kriss Kross?"* — I overhear a
> tormented man   I have no answer, no
> clue   just an ironic smirk, betrayer
> of my inner lie.

...and you might try to get a good look-see
at yourself

Booked into night   there   you   are
& you are not there

& under that, the obvious
mantle of paranoid rush
dishes out hard facts:
Who Are You???

You are not: Alicia Keys or
the New Jersey Knowbody that I am.

From where I recline
a viaduct becomes an elaborate
symbol of continuity

A dog is on the porch
in someone's white
domestic life

but not for me.

That certain sort of half-life
is plot-driven

I'm not a leek-wielding nationalist, though
my better parts derive from a minor prophet
and a faked Welsh lineage.

My belated lapse into subaltern poetics
makes me a little magnetic worker
& a part-time squirming referee.

Take this drift
of talk, normal
even plain speech. Use it
as evidence that
there's some brain
at work who has
been salt mining
for years. No trust
in the sleep salve
that puts things into
night play. Now face facts:
no angels have visited
a Jew in eons, *my dumb luck*
— got to depend on an innate
stealth, & there's just no morphine
in Christ-relief.

It's August 2006
and I'm stepping onto
the gum spot pavement
of Hoboken. With the Palisades
looming, I tune into the hemispheric
throb of the Lincoln Tunnel helix
and noise cars stalled
above weedy King's Bluff

And inside them jalopies:
men & women thumb drumming
steering wheels, daydreaming
disreputable thoughts
        & I'd bet a soda cracker

they'd rather be anywhere
than in that totem of false alarms
while faint silvery ozone
cooks up like Crisco
above Manhattan.

So, this brings us
to the problem
of incongruity
& artifice.

            People seem
              to have withdrawn
              into their own histories
              to find meaning.

            Does it mean that my
              sad life should be imbedded
              into the "work"
              crushed into a "poem"?

& just **what is** this
much **talked-about**
"imagination" except
the memory
of the good things
we ate as children.

I try to be a man of grief and fits
but my only possessions make me a
trivial vice-president of fog.

Nothing on the radio.
And only bus transfers on
the manifest list
in my cargo pants.

"A shenere un besere velt"
— a more beautiful & better world:
slogan of the Workman's Circle that Grandpa Jack
belonged to   People calling one another "*Comrade*"   Mayday
Bear Mountain picnics with Sidney Hillman's oratory
as actual entertainment   & I'm **so** nostalgic for that which
I never experienced.

                    Once comic North Korea now
a member in good standing of the **Axis O' Evil**   Memory
of attending study groups on "Juche" (*self-reliance?*)

& was it true
that Great Helmsman Kim Il Sung's face
was the desert at the bottom
of every North Korean's emptied soup bowl?

Gobs of storm fills Kill Van Kull with fog,
snaps me back to Carl-the-Maoist witnessing a Nor'easter
out the window of his girlfriend's Buick: **"WHAT-A-DAY!!**
I WOULDN'T WISH THIS ON A TROTSKYITE!"

MEMORIES OF A COLLEGE COMRADE

As I was discussing my attempts
to unshackle myself
from 9-to-5 work
and into
the freelance life
he cut me off:
"Joel, why don't you
stop this writing crap
*and get a **Real** job!"*

I didn't have an answer, really.
Though I did drop him a postcard
with the stark **"ET TU, LOUIE?"**

That was nine years ago just 26
years past our days debating
Gramsci over vend-o-mat dinners
& the last time we ever spoke
to each other.

A SON OF SILENCE

Hidden injuries of class?

He believed he could create a tornado
by flushing a toilet. He ate paper money, drank soapy
dish water, left golf clubs at synagogues
& collected JFK gas station tumblers. In his work for the CIA

he attempted to make cats organic eavesdropping drones
by implanting a listening device with the tail as antennae.

Problem: the cat would walk off the job when hungry.

Solution: a hunger "override" was implanted.

> When the improved acoustic cat was let out of the van
> *"A Yellow Cab ran over the operative"*.

Verdict: "In a real foreign situation,
the spy cat would not be practical."

THE GRAMSCI BLUES

In every era,
some blue collar American works
on her elocution skills, while
others continue to shout back orders from
behind the metal menu board
on a drive-thru line
                    but all that grasping at class position
doesn't seem to work.

For your inspection, here is a summary
of Professor Ronaldo Perrucci's
Four Quadrants of Class Position:

1— social capital (who you know)
2—credential capital (where you received your degree)
3—income/consumption capital
&
4—investment capital (stocks and bonds)

Driving back from another "pass the hat" reading, my
friend cried out: "I'd love to sell out!

The trouble is, *I have
nothing to sell!*"

6:23 am Northeast Corridor train to Trenton
the Meadows settled in darkness
Casmir Pulaski's skyway cloaked
in a minor scholar's colors
                    & just up ahead, Newark's skyline
is turbinado sugar
in the dawning sky's java.

Welcome citizen into the absent ravine that's
North Jersey, where flames shoot from cat-crackers
& landfills are loaded with broken blades.

The conductor holds up three fingers
& silently points at me. I didn't do
it, whatever **it** is.

I'm in tune with nothing.
I play saluggi with my books.
I can't stand the way I live.

   But I get with these places
stuck on back roads
brewed from a complex provincialism
with inhabitants living their lives out
on faint wishes
that fuel their lovely worlds.

So, what's left for me
but the sheer abandon
of watching the man across the aisle

debark at Metuchen
clutching a plush toy angelfish
into the washings of Jersey rain.

His dentist looked at his bleeding gums & scolded:
"Mitch, you got a bad case of *NYAMs* —

New York Adult Malnutrition

— the Big Mac is **not** a food group."

Why do some words live & some words

croak?   *"Shoe-icide bomber"*, **R.I.P.** I splash
invisible brown ink on imaginary rice paper
in a brief reverie for some short term diddy-wah-diddy.

Now, a shout-out to across-the-Passaic's Pulaski Skyway
— wrecked by Orson Welles, praised by Woody Guthrie
& still sentinel above the Meadowland's

industrial sublime.

Jersey Devil: he chilling in the Pine Barrens.
Itchy-trigger State Troopers at a Formica counter
inside a Route 22 Diner, Independence Day junkies
zip past, SUVs loaded with southland **M-80s.**

Me, **me?** *What's my story?*
I dress the poultry in black corduroy
and budding dictators in sans-a-belt slacks.
Louise Bogan, Howlin' Wolf and the other Joel Lewis at
the jug-handle turn, locked in a haiku contest, dreaming
nothing but secret radios.

At the portal to the PATH's
Hoboken terminal the Bengali owners
of the shabby, unnamed newsstand sell
murder poison   sports heroin   & shorn narratives
to the pleasant white breakfast clientele.

Heat wave breaks. Riverside homeless
take up begging posts and Wall Street djinns
scoop up the late financial news.

Other processes gum-up the wakeful mind:
Sen-Sen. Daily lotto talismans. What
a great day. Tourist boat
saunters up the Hudson. We don't

remain what we are. We don't
remain one of us. Taxis
line up as rush hour wanes. The steam
rising from a young woman's
Starbucks cup is my text
for the morning meditation
on **"gelt"**.

I have learnt by heart the lessons of the "fuck you!"
screamed like a baldie's lament in the Hoboken night.
The fake kidding aggression that's
mucilage for the casual male bonding
passing for friendship in these flinty days.

For 20 years I have watched Benny Tudino's pizza men
play an Albanian version of "**the dozens**"
"AH! I'LL KILL <u>YOU!!</u>"
"HAH! I KILL YOU FIRST, <u>MOTHERFUCK!!!</u>"
as they lob pepperoni disks upon slices
the size of a Panamanian jockey's torso.

G. Lakoff suggests that metaphors shape worldview
as in: "We must struggle for peace"
or: "the war on crime." **Fuck it!** In a tee-shirt
embroidered by sunshine, I advance into this
jack shit world of fake commerce.

Heavy Jesus has no mortgage on me.
I lack the ceremonial garments.
I mix the clarified butter with Crisco.
I'm not a gabbai.
And possess no high collar or antic wide brim.

The half-ruined cities of New Jersey
are at the core of my regional gestures
against insufficient nightmares
& the soft tyranny of bus schedules.

Generals go to the front room.
A stew of the old forces

back in the National Saddle
as my kimosabes and comrades

survive on unemployment checks
while I grow a spare head...

& it still won't help balance
midnight and the actual rain.

Dump some false drama
on tonight's donut shop:

Art Pepper over the speakers   he long out of
nine-cat lives   this pacified landscape

full of acts repeated in ignorance.
Call it: "the job"   I am not Tonto

but make it up in other ways.
Mute street lamps

swallow up
my echoed medium.

Tim Daly, "Depressed Highway, Routes 1&9," 27" x 39",
charcoal and pastel on paper, 1981. Collection of Sheilah
Scully-Daly, Hoboken, N.J.

FROM THE WAYNE SHORTER/SARAH VAUGHAN LIGHT RAIL STATION

Who doesn't eat lunch and board the streetcar
with his hired cigarette and his pocket-edition pain?
— *Cesar Vallejo*

1.

Kids don't kick cans for fun anymore
in America. Last night on
the Discovery Channel: program
after program about killer sharks
& their disfigured human victims.

2.

I have a Cibachrome postcard
of what I imagined my world to be,
age: indefinite. ***Damm you sharks!!***
Alchemy of the new generation of energy drinks.
His religion forbade fine French wines.

3.

I like exploring the mindset
of extreme expediency. The excitement of weekend
riders as the light rail train is sighted
across the prow of the minor league ballpark.
Sleepy "Brick City" as dreamed in Amiri's off-hours.

4.

I know where the rogue squirrels go.
Bald man talking into a tiny cell phone: " *I voted*
with my dog for the first time, which was
interesting." As a Paterson bound bus passes by,
Big Mac tumbleweeds roll into Military Park.

5.

Two dogs barking. Not at each
other, but in the plain manner that
might get each a soup bone
in the tenderest districts
of Newark.

6.

Into the inbound car: much heat, muted
noise, too much light. Read the letter section
in **Tikkun:** *"Instead of God, the Reform Rabbi
gave our congregation meteorology."*
My in-transit snack: cold yellow egg rolls.

7.

Newark: like watching fire ants on the doorjamb
in the loft of a retired physics professor.
New podcast: *"Picture your husband with
a whiter body."* All my actions are self-made prisons.
In a nutshell: I am ignorant of the causes of asymmetry.

8.

Down-the-street's Passaic: the only American
river capable of giving its fish-tenants
rug burns. Stagnant street furniture along Broad Street.
I told her last night: when you add it up, all I'm writing about
is electricity and gravity and birds.

9.

Graffiti on the walls of the Mulberry Street portal:
WE'LL MISS YOU BROTHER ED BRADLEY —- **ZEKE'S KREWE**
Good ideas slide off my egg roll stained polo shirt. Another wailing baby.
Newark at the end of Veterans Day. Thoughts of cold paella.
Writing is a gift to the crowded parts of my head.

10.

When bad people call my cell phone, it warns me
by playing a Bobby Timmons ring tone. Daydreaming
is the wobbly safety valve of a capitalist society. Sheer spiritual
volume of light rail wheels as we enter a curve. What this view
lacks: the green parole of trees.

11.

First whispers of the inevitable in Brick City:
"Do you want me to carry your kashi??" says
a woman in cottonwood bud skirt to her child.
I brought along a copy of the selected Yeats for no good reason.
Ahmad Jamal's "Billy Boy" in the headphones.

12.

Richard Nixon wore a tie to bed. Newark's
Penn Station in the not-that-distant "bad days"
was nicknamed **Mugger's Paradise.** I'm time stamped,
too old for recreational fare beating. I write.
Go blank. Scratch. Fiddle with the Nano. Stare out.

13.

Inside Penn Station's PATH train platform, I hear
native op-ed: "THAT RACIST KRAMER! I'LL
NEVER WATCH SEINFELD AGAIN!!!
Newsstand kiosk: *Hash browns for the winter solstice?* **That**
Martha Stewart! A river, the Passaic again, ahead in sunset shimmer.

<u>CODA</u>

There are times when I think it isn't quite
kosher to be sitting on the backseat chatting-up
women who aren't on the train. And it **does**
turn into a special kind of haunted
local news. But by and large, I dig it.

JAYWALKING ACROSS THE RED SEA

"I think we agree, the past is over." — G. W. Bush

Somewhere out there
someone is passing out
gas masks. But
"somewhere" is not
"no place" and it's occupied
by people closer
to our faces then
we'd believe.

Someplace in the world:
Banknotes are stacked.
Bonds are tallied.
Someplace is beneath
the floorboards. We drive
us. No calm life of roots.

We no longer "work".
We just amuse ourselves
with the "labor" to which
we're condemned. Our hands
are made of water. I don't know
how to explain this

but I have the foreboding
of a defective digital watch. And
all my reading
and all my lemon annotations
amount to daydreams guided
by a sweaty docent.

Another, better, man walks in his sleep
and aesthetes admire
his complete precision. **YO! All hail
the sleepwalker!** — the last
autonomous, self-actualized
Western artifact.

Covered over in duct tape, I come
into this old world naked. I was raised
to be adaptable to both cheapness
and achievement, but settled into
this clearing with
an adjustment disorder.
Should I invest in happenstance, *bud?*
— chains drop from an application of gravity.

Back again with "this",
with "these states" and all
held together with the drift
& persistence of me, *oy!*, Son
of Greenhorn. A halo
of flies mistakes my head
for a planet of shit. I try to feel
lucky despite many violations.

And if I go native, celebrate
 "Buy Nothing Day", will
"Das Big Ship Kapital" slow? I mean,
 can rounding out my Working Assets bill
mend our world? What can I do
with these hands of water?

A poet & her son are having dinner
at a Boston Market. "The eyelid
has its own storm," she tells me
forking faux-wild rice. This
dullard's walk is not without
value, but it lacks the melodrama
expected via TV's abstracting
emphasis on crap. Strange signals
as the artificial lighting
tapers off. More fare fed
into the fare box. Hoboken in all its
quotidian splendour.

No spiritual contamination here,
bwana. And too many dads
in ESPN-stupor nesting
in haunted mocha armchairs.
I'd like to think I "help out"
 in the general repair work,
warming up to truants & their
frazzled families of origin

but who I kid ? Diaspora Joe
here on the Social Control beat. Just
another sunset in this city
of unhappy waitresses. And look
who is passing me by: *People of Hudson County.*

young women clad
in corporate picnic t-shirts, old
guys yapping Italian, one
Lutheran minister named Helga
& a pack of renegade Cub Scouts
on skateboards. And all it does
for me is stir up coffee jitters
and memories of loud noise.

Storm clouds again   a smudge
of damson above the Lincoln Tunnel helix
shifting pink streaks beneath that
                         & way below: the world-that-is called
rush hour   folks in BMWs, jalopies, buses & vans getting
ready to walk the American gangplank
again   I escape by boat but remain a fellow cog
in the volitional economy
of the brightways, my
helping profession
a part of a procession
prophesized in the Book of Lacks.

a long flowing garment
long sleeves
ankle length

My caftan swells under
the brainwork involved
in managing the usual mediated day.
The house elder intones:
"Intuition antedates all creation." And
I think: "Who is **he** kidding?" then
saunter off to the corny portals
of the old Hudson Tubes
on a cold coastal Tuesday

worn, with
conflicting parties
to settle differences

PATH

How much does the face change
through the permutations
of a weekday? I seem unrecognizable
to you, you & **you**   but that doesn't
shame me. My white noise kvetching goes up
into the urban air that's always
shouting someone's given name.

                    Serendipity. Chance. Daily life.
And that might be just
enough/all there is.
                        No revelation, salvation or election
except in the allegory & music
of the passed-down cyclorama.

Major prophet   minor prophet   not doing a thing about it.
Calibrating the accuracy of the moment.